MICHELANGELO

First published in Great Britain
in Gollancz Children's Paperbacks 1993
by Victor Gollancz
A Cassell imprint
Villiers House
41/47 Strand
London WC2N 5JE

Copyright © Aladdin Books Limited 1993
An Aladdin Book
Designed and produced by
Aladdin Books Limited
28 Percy Street
London W1P 9FF

Design: David West Children's Book Design
Researched by Gillian Bainbridge BA Hons, ATC

A catalogue record for this book
is available from the British Library

The moral right of the author has been asserted

ISBN 0 575 05681 9

Special thanks to: The Bridgeman Art Library; Staatliche Graphische
Sammlung, Munich; Scala, Florence. The publishers have made every
effort to contact all the relevant copyright holders and apologise for
any omissions that may have inadvertently been made.

Printed in Belgium

Famous Children

MICHELANGELO

TONY HART & SUSAN HELLARD

GOLLANCZ CHILDREN'S PAPERBACKS
LONDON

In the town of Caprese in Italy, during the spring of 1475, Francesca Buonarroti gave birth to her second son.

"We'll call him Michelangelo," announced the boy's father proudly.

Soon afterwards Lodovico Buonarroti's job as Mayor of Caprese came to an end and the family packed up their belongings to return

home. The baby Michelangelo travelled with his parents to the family home in Florence and from there to Settignano, a village outside the town, where he lived with his nurse.

The countryside all around Settignano was very rich in stone. Quarries were everywhere, mined by stone-cutters and sculptors.

Little Michelangelo grew up surrounded by chisels and hammers as his nurse's father and husband were both stonemasons.

"You will soon know all about stone-carving, Michelangelo," joked his nurse.

As Michelangelo played amongst the stones and quarries of Settignano, his family grew. Three more sons were born to Francesca and Lodovico. But sadly, when Michelangelo was six years old, his mother died.

Four years later Lodovico married again. Michelangelo returned to Florence to join the family. He shared a gloomy house with his father, his stepmother, four brothers and an uncle.

Michelangelo's father didn't earn much money. Some of his sons had to help out and were sent to work for silk and wool merchants. Michelangelo, though, went to school.

When his father realized that Michelangelo spent his time at school drawing instead of studying, he became very angry.

"You are wasting time on art. You will never make any money for yourself or for the family."

Michelangelo had been given the chance to become a scholar but all he wanted to do was draw!

He became friendly with a local boy called Francesco Granacci. Francesco had been sent as a boy to learn the art of painting from Domenico Ghirlandaio, a famous local artist.

"You have great talent," said Francesco when he saw Michelangelo's work. "I shall help you with your studies."

Michelangelo was delighted.

Every day Francesco would bring one of Domenico's drawings for Michelangelo to study and copy.

Michelangelo became better and better until his father realized that there was no hope of forcing his son to give up drawing.

"I give in, you shall put these talents to good use and learn art properly," sighed his father.

Michelangelo couldn't wait to tell Francesco that he would soon be joining him.

Michelangelo became apprenticed to Domenico when he was 13 years old. He learned the difficult technique of "fresco", painting on wet plaster.

"This is excellent, Michelangelo. You are improving at an astonishing rate," gasped Domenico.

He soon allowed the eager young apprentice to work with him on public frescos. This was considered a great honour for Michelangelo.

Michelangelo was still only 13 when he painted a kneeling figure in Domenico's fresco of The Baptism of Christ.

One day Michelangelo watched an apprentice copy a drawing of Domenico's.

Age 13

Michelangelo took the drawing and using a thicker pen he went over the lines and improved it.

"You are better than our master!" exclaimed the apprentice.

Domenico himself was often to be surprised by Michelangelo. One day when they were working together in a chapel, Michelangelo started to sketch.

He drew what he saw around him – the scaffolding, trestle tables, stools and materials, as well as all the men working there. When Domenico saw what Michelangelo had done he was astonished.

"This boy knows more than I do!" he shouted with excitement.

Michelangelo was always searching for new ideas. He made a perfect copy in pen and ink of an engraving by a famous German artist. It showed St Anthony being tormented by devils.

Michelangelo wanted to add colour to the drawing.

"I need some help with the colours of the demons. I know – I'll look at some fish to see the fantastic colours of the scales."

Michelangelo also made excellent copies of the works of other famous artists such as Giotto and Masaccio.

"I shall tinge them with smoke, then they will look old and exactly like the original drawings," thought Michelangelo. And they did.

News of the boy's talents began to spread.

Age 13

Age 13

Lorenzo the Magnificent lived in the Medici Palace in Florence. He was the ruler of Florence and a great art lover and collector. He sent a message to Domenico.

"Send me your best pupils to study with the famous sculptor, Bertoldo, in my Sculpture Garden."

Domenico felt very honoured by Lorenzo's request and immediately sent, among others, both Michelangelo and Francesco. Michelangelo was fascinated by the wonderful sculptures he saw there. He longed for the chance to make one himself.

Within a few days, Michelangelo began a marble copy of an antique faun's head which he found in the garden. The face was very old, with wrinkles. It had a damaged nose and a laughing mouth.

This was the first time Michelangelo had worked with marble but the copy was excellent. Lorenzo was walking through the garden, watching the boys at work. He saw the faun and was very impressed.

Then Lorenzo noticed that Michelangelo had given the faun a tongue and all its teeth. He laughed and said,

"But you should have known that old men never have all their teeth, some of them are always missing."

Michelangelo took this criticism very seriously and, anxious to please Lorenzo, he broke one of the faun's teeth and dug a hole in the gum so that it looked as if the tooth had fallen out.

"Please Sir, is this better?" he asked hopefully.

Lorenzo laughed even more.

"It is perfect!" he exclaimed.

Lorenzo decided to help young Michelangelo. He sent for the boy's father and asked whether Michelangelo could stay at the Palace.

"I shall look after him as if he is one of my own sons," he promised.

His father willingly agreed and Michelangelo, at 15 years old, was given his own room at the Palace and ate all his meals with Lorenzo's family. And most important of all, he was given the keys to the Sculpture Garden.

Michelangelo worked hard. Other students began to envy his talent. A friend of Michelangelo's became so jealous that he punched him on the nose, breaking it. Michelangelo had a scar for the rest of his life.

During his stay at the Medici Palace, Michelangelo carved many pieces of marble.

"His work is so beautiful that it is almost impossible to

Age 16

believe it's the work of a young man and not a great master," said Lorenzo.

In 1492, when Michelangelo was 17 years old, Lorenzo died. Michelangelo was filled with sorrow at the death of his generous friend.

Age 16

Michelangelo returned to live with his father, now in Rome. The following year he bought a large block of marble and carved a statue of "Hercules", two and a half metres high, in memory of Lorenzo de Medici the Magnificent.

Lorenzo's son, Piero de Medici, was a great friend to Michelangelo too, and would ask his advice about buying antiques.

One winter it snowed heavily in Florence and Piero asked him,

"Can you make a statue out of snow?"

Michelangelo made a beautiful snow sculpture in Piero's courtyard. Everyone was amazed and Piero praised Michelangelo so highly that even Lodovico had to admit that his son was someone very special indeed.

Michelangelo lived for nearly 90 years and created some of the most beautiful works of art the world has ever seen.